COCKTAILS

FOR THE FOUR SEASONS

BY JENNY PARK
& TERI LYN FISHER

PETER PAUPER PRESS, INC.
White Plains, New York

PETER PAUPER PRESS
Fine Books and Gifts Since 1928

OUR COMPANY

In 1928, at the age of twenty-two, Peter Beilenson began printing books on a small press in the basement of his parents' home in Larchmont, New York. Peter—and later, his wife, Edna—sought to create fine books that sold at "prices even a pauper could afford."

Today, still family owned and operated, Peter Pauper Press continues to honor our founders' legacy—and our customers' expectations—of beauty, quality, and value.

COCKTAILS

FOR THE FOUR SEASONS

TABLE OF CONTENTS

INTRODUCTION

D o you remember ordering your very first cocktail? Undoubtedly, you were probably surrounded by your other newly legal-aged drinking friends. Staring at the back bar—lined with a multitude of fancy labeled bottles in all different shapes and sizes—you might have felt intimidated and overwhelmed at this first-time decision! And maybe— just maybe—you ended up with a drink that was less than what you had hoped for, or was just plain gross!

Well, friends, you're all grown up now and the power to please your palate is completely in your own hands— in fact, you're *literally* holding it in your hands right now by holding this book! We have crafted a bounty of delicious cocktail recipes for you to enjoy—cocktails we've made for parties and ones we've created to wind down from a hard day.

Living in Los Angeles, we are spoiled with a wonderful selection of fresh produce. Whether it's taking advantage of those sweet and juicy ruby red grapefruits in early spring or those mouth-watering strawberries in summer, we've concocted seasonal drinks to be enjoyed all year round with friends and family. Cheers!

—Jenny & Teri

BEHIND-THE-BAR BASICS

Start out your cocktail connoisseurship in style! From glassware to garnishes, and savory to sweet syrups—we've got you covered with these behind-the-bar basics.

KNOW YOUR BARWARE

It's always great to have an assortment of glassware on hand. The vessel for your drink can make a statement—from classic to casual. On the next few pages, we've included descriptions for basic glassware and bar tools that we've used in this book, but there's a wide variety of shapes and sizes available out there so feel free to switch it up! (Please note we've listed general capacity sizes, but they can vary.)

1. Muddler
2. Coupe
3. Highball
4. Cocktail Strainer
5. Snifter
6. Julep Cup
7. Mug
8. Half-Pint
9. Punch Bowl Mug
10. Collins
11. Cocktail Shaker
12. Champagne Flute
13. Bar Spoon
14. Cocktail/Martini Glass
15. Pint Glass
16. Double Old Fashioned
17. Stemless Wine Glass
18. Jigger
19. Old Fashioned
20. Milk Punch Cup

Bar Spoon: These long-handled spoons are used for mixing drinks in tall glasses, as well as creating layered drinks by various techniques (often involving pouring a liquid over the back of the spoon so that it enters the glass slowly and doesn't mix in with the other drink components).

Champagne Flute: Perfect for bubbly drinks, this long, narrow bowled glass helps to keep the bubbles contained and has a more narrow top than bottom. It comes with or without a stem. (6 to 8 oz.)

Cocktail/Martini Glass: This iconic cocktail glass is home to classics like martinis and cosmopolitans. The glass has a cone-shaped bowl, which allows the aroma to drift up to the drinker as they sip. They usually are stemmed, but are also available stemless. (4.5 oz.)

Cocktail Shaker: In order to be an authentic cocktail connoisseur you simply must have a cocktail shaker (most of our recipes require one). Shakers are available in either 2- or 3-piece sets, some with built-in strainers. They're used to vigorously shake the cocktails (often with ice) before straining them into serving glasses.

Cocktail Strainer: Used in tandem with a cocktail shaker, this tool is used to strain ice from a drink after it's been shaken. It's essential for serving a "straight up" drink—which is a drink shaken with ice to slightly chill it, but served in a glass without any ice.

Collins: Because of their small-surface narrow tops and lean long cylindrical figures, these glasses are great for carbonated drinks like our Sweet Citrus Fizz. They keep the fizz in! (10 to 14 oz.)

Coupe: Traditionally used as a champagne glass, the coupe is now more often seen holding a variety of cocktails (we like to use them for drinks served without ice). Its broad bowl, which sits upon a short stem, allows more bubbles to escape, so we don't recommend using it for carbonated drinks. (8 to 12 oz.)

Double Old Fashioned: Generally the same shape as an old fashioned glass, but taller—for when you just need double the strength! (12 to 16 oz.)

Half-Pint: Same cone-shape as the original pint glass, but—you guessed it—its capacity is half that of a full pint glass. (8 to 10 oz.)

Highball: While similar in height to Collins glasses, these glasses are slightly shorter and wider. They're usually used for drinks that have a higher ratio of "mixer" to liquor (e.g. our Raspberry Mojito, which has a higher ratio of club soda to rum). That's right—all those years you were drinking Rum & Cokes out of red plastic cups, you should have been drinking them from highballs! (8 to 12 oz.)

Jigger: A handy measuring tool to keep at the bar, a jigger usually has two different cone-shaped compartments. One most often holds 1.5 oz., while the other holds a fraction or multiple of that.

Julep Cup: This handsome cup isn't just pretty to look at—its silver or pewter material serves an important purpose. When a cold drink is added, a frost will form on the outside of the cup and will help keep the contents nice and chilly! (8 to 12 oz.)

Milk Punch Cup: Perfect for slushy chilled drinks, this silver or pewter cup helps retain the milk's natural chill.

Muddler: The essential mojito-maker tool! This device "muddles" up ingredients (like herbs, fruit, sugar, and spices) to release their flavors and allow them to seep into your tasty beverages.

Mug: There's a wide range of mugs out there in the world, but the most defining feature is that they're designed to hold hot beverages. They usually have handles, or are specially insulated—like the mug tumblers we used in our Vanilla Bean Irish Coffee recipe. They're larger than teacups and more casual. (12 oz.)

Old Fashioned: Primarily used for serving small (and strong) cocktails over ice, these wide-brimmed short tumblers are a staple in every bar. (6 to 10 oz.)

Pint Glass: Probably one of the most commonly-used bar glasses, the pint glass is primarily used to serve beer. Usually they're an inverted cone-shape (with the pointy tops cut off of course!). True to its name, the U.S. pint glass holds 16 ounces, although if you're in Britain the pint glass usually holds 20 ounces.

Punch Bowl Mug: We're suckers for punch bowl sets—they come in so many different colors, shapes, and sizes. Although the punch bowl mug that we have pictured on page 9 has a handle, some accompanying glasses may be more like tumblers. Punch bowls are typically large enough to hold at least 32 ounces, while the individual glasses range from about 6 to 8 oz.

Snifter: It's not a hard reach to see where this glass gets its name—the wide bowl lets some of the liquor release while the narrow top traps the aroma and allows the user to "sniff" the contents. Traditionally this short-stemmed glass is used for warm spirits, such as brandy, but we've shaken it up a bit and used this fun glass for some of our cool cocktails like the Roasted Strawberry and Jalapeño Freezer! (6 to 8 oz.)

Stemless Wine Glass: Wine glasses come in a variety of shapes with different "bowl" sizes to allow for different flavor concentrations and aromas to arise from each wine. These stemless versions are becoming quite the trend and can be used for a variety of drinks.

SIMPLE GARNISHES TO DRESS UP
YOUR DRINKS

While choosing the type of glass for your drink sets the visual mood, a garnish can really take it up a notch. Some of our drinks feature special, unique garnishes (their specific instructions are included within the individual recipes), but here are some tried-and-true basics that you'll see repeated throughout the book.

Citrus Twists

Wash the lemons, limes, oranges, or other citrus fruit. Hold the fruit firmly in the palm of your hand. With a paring knife, gently cut a strip of peel, and slowly roll the fruit in your hand. When you have a peel of your desired length, cut it off and then carefully roll it into a spiral (without breaking it). Give it a gentle squeeze and release.

Citrus Wedges

Wash the lemons, limes, oranges, or other citrus fruit. Slice the fruit in half lengthwise. Place each half flat-side down, and cut lengthwise into 3 to 4 wedges.

Citrus Wheels

Wash the lemons, limes, oranges, or other citrus fruit. Cut off the ends. Cut crosswise into ⅛ to ¼-inch slices. The wheels can remain whole, or be cut into half or quarter-slices.

SIMPLE SYRUP SECRET

If you've ever experienced a deliciously sweet drink and can't quite figure out how they did it—it was most likely done by using a simple syrup! Here's a basic recipe, with some fun variations.

BASIC SIMPLE SYRUP RECIPE
MAKES 8 OUNCES

INGREDIENTS
1 cup superfine sugar (granulated is okay)
8 ounces water

1. Pour the sugar and water into a small saucepan and stir together. Place over medium heat and simmer until all the sugar has dissolved, 5 to 7 minutes. Remove from the heat and set aside until completely cooled.

2. For variations *(see page 17)*: Once the sugar has dissolved, remove from the heat, add the flavoring ingredients, cover, and allow to steep for at least 1 hour (and not more than 4 hours). Strain and set aside until completely cooled and ready to use.

3. To store: Pour the mixture into an airtight container and refrigerate for up to 1 week.

VARIATIONS:

- **basil simple syrup:** 15 basil leaves, loosely torn
- **dill simple syrup:** 2 sprigs dill, lightly massaged
- **ginger simple syrup:** 2-inch piece fresh ginger, peeled and thinly sliced
- **jalapeño simple syrup:** 3 jalapeños, seeded and quartered
- **lavender simple syrup:** 4 sprigs lavender, lightly massaged
- **lemongrass simple syrup:** 1 2-inch piece fresh lemongrass, thinly sliced
- **mint simple syrup:** 12 mint leaves, loosely torn
- **rosemary simple syrup:** 3 sprigs rosemary, needles lightly massaged
- **tamarind simple syrup:** ¼ cup tamarind paste
- **thyme simple syrup:** 8 sprigs thyme, lightly massaged

A NOTE ABOUT THIS BOOK

It's always a good idea to read a recipe all the way though before the imbibing party begins! Make sure you have all of the necessary ingredients and tools on hand so that you're not running around freaking out about lemon twists while your guests are awaiting their drinks! Speaking of garnishes, we've included our favorites for each drink, but of course you should feel free to experiment. If we've topped off our drink with one lemon slice, that doesn't mean you can't use two. As such, many of the garnish measurements provided are approximations—so do what you feel is most visually appealing. The same goes for choosing glassware. We've included our suggestions, but of course there are no strict guidelines. Where applicable, we've made recommendations for specific brands of ingredients that we like, but you can always use what is most easily available to you. (There's a glossary of ingredients in the back of the book to help guide your way.) Sometimes when you can't find a specific ingredient that a recipe calls for, you end up substituting with an alternative and *boom* . . . a new drink is born. Bottoms up!

SPRING RECIPES

We always are very excited for spring—it's like waking up from a deep slumber. The flowers are starting to bloom and the scent of nature is in the air. What better way to kick this season into high gear than with some fresh, light cocktails! From the crisp **Rosé-Dill Spritzer** to the floral **Lavender Limoncello**, these drinks will satisfy your spring tooth!

HONEY BEAR

SERVES 4

This bourbon-based cocktail, infused with natural honey and spices has an added splash of fresh Meyer lemon juice to cut through the overall sweetness.

INGREDIENTS

8 ounces bourbon
3 tablespoons honey, warmed
2 ounces Tuaca
1 Meyer lemon, juiced
2 ounces maraschino cherry juice*
8 dashes orange bitters

GARNISH

4 maraschino cherries

1. In a small bowl, stir together the bourbon and warmed honey until the honey dissolves.

2. Pour the honey-bourbon, Tuaca, Meyer lemon juice, and maraschino cherry juice into a cocktail shaker and fill it with ice.

3. Shake for 1 minute and divide into four half-pint glasses filled with ice.

4. Top each drink with two dashes of orange bitters and garnish with a maraschino cherry. Serve.

*Maraschino cherry juice can be found in specialty stores, supermarkets, and online.

ROSÉ-DILL SPRITZER

SERVES 4

Wine cocktails have a bad reputation for being dated and uninspiring drinks, but we're here to change all that! The addition of the savory dill, infused into the sweet rosé, creates a really great balance between flavors.

INGREDIENTS

8 ounces dill simple syrup (see page 16)
1 (750 ml) bottle rosé wine
12 ounces club soda

GARNISH

4 sprigs fresh dill

1. Pour the syrup, wine, and club soda into a large pitcher filled with ice. Stir.

2. Pour the spritzer into four half-pint glasses or stemless white wine glasses.

3. Garnish each cocktail with sprigs of dill and serve.

ROSEMARY-GRAPEFRUIT COOLER

SERVES 4

This cocktail blends the sweetness of grapefruit with the bold flavors of rosemary to create a uniquely refreshing drink. Broiling or grilling the grapefruit halves for a couple minutes before juicing them adds a subtle smoky finish to this rad beverage, and we urge you to try it out from time to time.

INGREDIENTS

16 ounces reposado tequila
8 ounces rosemary simple syrup (see page 16)
3 ruby red grapefruits, juiced (about 1⅔ cups)

GARNISH

4 rosemary sprigs

1. Place the tequila, syrup, and grapefruit juice into a cocktail shaker and fill it with ice (you might have to make this in two batches). Shake for about 1 minute.

2. Add ice to four half-pint glasses and pour the contents of the shaker into each glass until full.

3. Garnish each cocktail with a sprig of fresh rosemary and serve.

RUBY RED AND TONICS

SERVES 4

Our fun take on gin and tonics with fresh ruby red grapefruit juice and one of our very favorite cordials, St-Germain! The elderflower liqueur adds a delicate flavor to our truly tasty version of gin and tonics.

INGREDIENTS

4 ounces gin
4 ounces St-Germain, or any elderflower liqueur
1 ruby red grapefruit, juiced (about ⅔ cup)
12 ounces tonic water

GARNISH

Ruby red grapefruit wheels (quartered), from
*   1 grapefruit (see page 14)*

1. Pour the gin, St-Germain, and grapefruit juice into a cocktail shaker and fill it with ice. Shake for 1 minute.

2. Strain the mixture into four coupe glasses and finish with tonic water.

3. Garnish each glass with a quartered grapefruit wheel. Serve.

SALTY DOG
SERVES 4

Our favorite thing about this cocktail is the yummy grapefruit zest and salt rim! It's a total game-changer for this awesomely simple drink!

INGREDIENTS
½ cup honey
⅓ cup kosher salt
4 grapefruits, zested
12 ounces gin
10 ruby red grapefruits, juiced

1. Spread the honey onto a plate in a thin layer. Combine the salt and grapefruit zest onto another plate and stir with a fork until completely combined.

2. Rim four double old fashioned glasses with a thin layer of honey, followed by the salt mixture. Set the prepared glasses aside until ready to use.

3. Place the gin and grapefruit juice into a cocktail shaker and fill it with ice (you might have to make this in two batches). Shake for about 1 minute.

4. Fill the prepared glasses with ice (or you can place one giant ice cube into each glass), and strain the contents of the shaker into each glass. Serve.

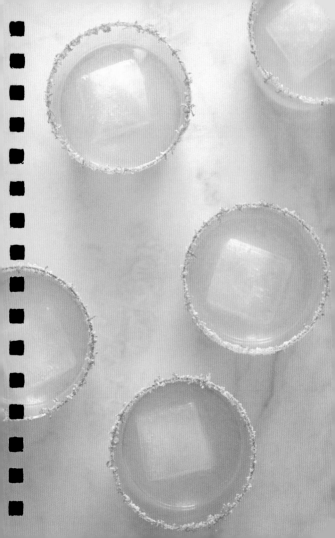

LAVENDER LIMONCELLO
SERVES 8

We turned this typical Italian liqueur into a not so typical splendor, by blending the citrus flavors with the sweet floral notes of lavender. Although some patience is required, it's totally worth the wait! This super fragrant and thirst-quenching cocktail is great for warm spring days. We highly recommend making this addicting drink by the pitcher!

INGREDIENTS

12 lemons, scrubbed
1 bottle (750ml) good quality vodka (minimum
  80 proof/40%)
12 ounces lavender simple syrup (see page 16)
24 ounces sparkling lemonade

GARNISH

8 fresh lavender sprigs
Lemon wheels, from 2 lemons (see page 14)

(CONTINUED)

1. Peel all of the lemons with a vegetable peeler or knife, removing as much pith (white stuff) as possible from the peels.

2. Thinly slice the peels and place them into a large jar (mason jars work great for this).

3. Pour the vodka over the peels, seal the jar, and allow the mixture to infuse in a cool, dry place for 2 to 3 weeks, shaking the mixture once every 2 days.

4. After 2 to 3 weeks have gone by, strain the vodka and lemon peel mixture. Stir the lavender simple syrup into the infused vodka.

5. Pour the mixture into eight Collins glasses, filled with ice, and top with the sparkling lemonade. Finish with lavender and lemon wheels. Serve.

SOJU BLOODY MARY

SERVES 4

It's always fun to turn your cocktail into a dual cocktail-snack, which is what we've done with our version of this typical breakfast beverage. We finish each of our spicy drinks with a sweet, skinned cherry tomato and a homemade pickled cocktail shrimp!

INGREDIENTS
Bloody Mary Mix:

1 14.5-ounce can whole tomatoes with juices

24 ounces pure tomato juice

3 tablespoons Worcestershire sauce

2 tablespoons Sriracha (or any hot sauce)

1½ tablespoons grated horseradish

2 teaspoons grated ginger

1 teaspoon kosher salt

1 teaspoon cracked black pepper

2 lemons, juiced

Alcohol:

12 ounces soju (or vodka)

GARNISH

Lemon wedges, from 1 lemon (see page 14)

4 pickled shrimp and cherry tomato skewers (see page 38 for recipe)

(CONTINUED)

1. Place all of the bloody mary mix ingredients into a blender and blend until smooth. Pour into a pitcher and chill in the refrigerator for at least 1 hour.

2. Divide the soju into four half-pint, or Collins glasses and top with ice.

3. Fill each glass with the bloody mary mix and stir together.

4. Add a lemon wedge to each glass and top with a shrimp and tomato skewer. Serve.

PICKLED SHRIMP AND CHERRY TOMATO SKEWERS

INGREDIENTS

12 cherry tomatoes

2 tablespoons minced parsley

4 sprigs thyme

¼ small red onion, thinly sliced

1 lemon, juiced

3 cloves garlic, lightly smashed

1½ tablespoons granulated sugar

1 tablespoon black peppercorns

2 teaspoons kosher salt

1½ teaspoons mustard seeds

1 teaspoon celery seeds

½ teaspoon all-spice berries

2 cups white wine vinegar

12 precooked shrimp

1 cup extra virgin olive oil

1. Fill a small pot with water and bring to a boil. While waiting for the water to boil, make an ice bath by pouring 2 cups of ice and 4 cups of water into a mixing bowl.

2. Gently score the twelve cherry tomatoes with a paring knife and carefully drop the tomatoes into the boiling water for about 30 seconds. Using a slotted spoon, quickly scoop the tomatoes out of the pot and into the ice bath. Allow the tomatoes to sit for 5 minutes in the ice bath.

3. Remove the tomatoes from the ice bath and skin them. Then roll each one in the parsley and set aside.

4. Place the thyme, onion, lemon juice, garlic, sugar, black peppercorns, salt, mustard seeds, celery seeds, all-spice berries, and white wine vinegar in a medium pot. Simmer over medium-low heat for 10 minutes.

5. Place the 12 shrimp into a nonreactive mixing bowl and pour the vinegar mixture over the shrimp. Allow the mixture to sit for 20 minutes. Then, whisk in the olive oil and allow the shrimp to sit for another 20 minutes.

6. Skewer the shrimp and cherry tomatoes onto cocktail picks. (Serve the leftovers on the side.)

SPIKED SHIRLEY TEMPLE

SERVES 4

We've turned one of our favorite childhood classics into a tasty, adult-friendly cocktail. Don't be fooled by the cute exterior, if you're not careful these drinks will totally get you sauced!

INGREDIENTS

4 ounces citrus vodka
4 ounces Luxardo, or any maraschino liqueur
8 ounces lemon-lime soda, chilled
*2 ounces maraschino cherry juice**

GARNISH

Maraschino cherries (optional)

1. Place the vodka and Luxardo into a cocktail shaker and fill it with ice.

2. Shake for 1 minute and strain the mixture into four coupe glasses.

3. Top each drink with the lemon-lime soda and finish with a drizzle of maraschino cherry juice.

4. Garnish each glass with a maraschino cherry, if using, and serve.

Maraschino cherry juice can be found in specialty stores, supermarkets, and online.

SUMMER RECIPES

Summer brings in a wonderful bounty of beautiful produce and ingredients, from fresh berries and honeydew melons to luscious, tropical pineapples. And with summer—let's face it—often comes some annoyingly hot days! Our favorite cure: sitting by the pool, sipping on a refreshing cocktail (can anyone say **Raspberry Mojito** or **Mint Julep**?), and not moving…like…for several hours.

BLACKBERRY AND LEMON DAIQUIRI

SERVES 2

We love blended cocktails, especially daiquiris, but not necessarily ones with artificially colored mystery syrups. Gross! Here we have a tasty daiquiri that uses frozen blackberries and fresh lemons to create a fun and boldly colored blended concoction!

INGREDIENTS

12 ounces frozen blackberries
6 lemons, juiced
6 ounces white rum
4 ounces coconut rum
4 ounces pineapple juice
2 tablespoons superfine sugar

GARNISH

2 mint sprigs
Lemon zest, from 1 lemon

1. Place all of the ingredients into a blender and purée until smooth. Pour into two snifters.

2. Garnish each with a sprig of mint and a sprinkle of lemon zest. Serve.

BROWN SUGAR CAIPIRINHA

SERVES 4

We took this popular and energizing Brazilian cocktail and tweaked the classic by muddling our limes with light brown sugar instead of cane sugar. A fun fact about this drink is that it originated as an elixir to aid in healing colds; once sugar was added to it, they dropped the garlic (yep, garlic!) and began serving it as a tasty social beverage.

INGREDIENTS

¼ cup light brown sugar
12 lime wedges (about 3 limes)
8 ounces cachaça
12 ounces club soda

GARNISH

Lime wedges, from 1 lime (see page 14)

1. Set out four stemless wine glasses or four double old fashioned glasses, and fill each with one tablespoon of sugar and three lime wedges. Muddle together.

2. Fill each glass with ice, top with the cachaça, and stir. Finish each cocktail with club soda.

3. Garnish with extra lime wedges. Serve.

CARIBBEAN SURPRISE

SERVES 4

Our obsession with unique flavor combinations and our affinity for lemongrass led us to blend this unique aromatic ingredient with the classic tropical flavors of pineapples and coconut rum—creating a sweet and sharp beverage, with hints of vanilla from the dash of Tuaca, a vanilla-citrus liqueur.

INGREDIENTS

12 ounces coconut rum
8 ounces lemongrass simple syrup (see page 16)
8 ounces coconut water
6 ounces pineapple juice
2 ounces Tuaca

GARNISH

4 lemongrass spears*

1. Place all of the ingredients into a large mason jar filled with ice. Shake for 1 minute. Strain the cocktail into four half-pint glasses filled with ice.

2. Garnish with lemongrass spears. Serve.

*Remove the tough, outer layers of the lemongrass stalks, and slice into about 4- to 5-inch spears. You may want to cut several small slits in the spears to release more of the lemon flavor.

CLASSIC BELLINI

SERVES 4

As lovers of prosecco and fresh fruit cocktails, this classic Italian aperitif is one of our favorite anytime drinks. The white peach puree is so light and smooth, and it's fun to adjust the amounts depending on your own personal taste.

INGREDIENTS

1 white peach, peeled, seeded, and chopped
1½ ounces all natural cherry juice (optional)
16 ounces prosecco

1. Place the peach into a food processor and purée until smooth. Pour into a liquid measuring cup and stir in the cherry juice, if using.

2. Divide the purée mixture into four champagne flutes and top each glass with the prosecco.

COCONUT RUM PUNCH
SERVES 12 TO 15

This drink is a staple for our summer parties because it's so easy to make for big groups. Everyone loves the tropical taste of this punch, and party goers are always impressed by the beautiful edible flower garnish.

INGREDIENTS
32 ounces ginger beer
24 ounces dark rum
16 ounces pineapple juice
12 ounces coconut rum
8 ounces yellow chartreuse
8 ounces Domaine de Canton, or any ginger liqueur
8 ounces passion fruit syrup*
5 oranges, juiced

GARNISH
Edible flowers
Orange wheels, from 2 oranges (see page 14)

1. Pour all of the ingredients into a punch bowl and stir. Fill with ice and continue to stir until fully combined.

2. Garnish with edible flowers and orange wheels. Serve.

*Passion fruit syrup can be found in specialty stores, supermarkets, and online.

DARK AND STORMY
SERVES 4

Ginger beer is one of our favorite refreshing drinks on its own. Naturally, we knew we would love a good Dark and Stormy. The kick of ginger at the end of each sip and the smooth taste the dark rum gives you—we love this drink to its core.

INGREDIENTS
6 ounces dark rum
4 ounces Domaine de Canton, or any ginger liqueur
1 lime, juiced
12 ounces ginger beer

GARNISH
Lime wheels, from 2 limes (see page 14)

1. Pour the rum, Domaine de Canton, and lime juice into a cocktail shaker filled with ice and shake for 1 minute.

2. Pour the mixture into four double old fashioned glasses filled with ice. Top each drink with ginger beer and stir.

3. Garnish with lime wheels. Serve.

GRILLED PEACH RUM PUNCH

SERVES 8

Sometimes as the end of summer approaches we hoard as much stone fruit as possible. Even after cutting up and freezing pounds upon pounds, we're usually still left with tons of ripe fruit! One way to use it all up, especially the peaches, is to grill and then purée them into a juice, creating a great base for this rum punch and many other yummy cocktails!

INGREDIENTS

20 ripe peaches, halved and pitted
3½ tablespoons extra virgin olive oil
24 ounces dark rum
16 ounces fresh key lime juice (30 to 40 key limes)
24 ounces club soda

GARNISH

Grilled peach slices, from 2 peaches (follow grilling instructions in step 1)
Extra virgin olive oil (enough to brush each side of the peach slices)
Key lime wheels, from 5 key limes (see page 14)

(CONTINUED)

1. Preheat a grill or grill pan over medium-high heat. Brush the peaches with the olive oil. Grill each peach, on each side, for 3 to 5 minutes.

2. Place the peaches into a blender and purée until smooth. Strain and pour the peach juice into a large punch bowl, along with the rum, lime juice, and club soda. Fill with ice and stir.

3. Ladle the punch into eight juice or punch glasses and garnish with a grilled peach slice and a couple of key lime wheels. Serve.

PINEAPPLE-THYME MAI-TAI

SERVES 4

Mai-Tai cocktails remind us of tropical vacations, tanning at the beach, and most of all the awesomely bad paper umbrellas that always seem to come with the drink! We've not only updated the flavors, but also the look by replacing the '80s-esque cocktail picks with cute pom-pom picks!

INGREDIENTS

2 oranges, juiced
5 sprigs thyme
8 ounces dark rum
4 ounces coconut rum
4 ounces pineapple juice
4 ounces maraschino cherry juice*

GARNISH

4 grilled pineapple wedges**
4 thyme sprigs
Maraschino cherry juice* (optional)

*Maraschino cherry juice can be found in specialty stores, supermarkets, and online.

**To prepare grilled pineapple wedges, first cut the pineapple into about ¼-inch slices. Then grill each side for about 3 minutes. Slice into triangle wedges.

(CONTINUED)

1. Pour the orange juice into a small bowl and drop in the thyme sprigs. Cover and allow the mixture to infuse for 1 hour, and then remove the thyme sprigs.

2. Pour the rums, pineapple juice, thyme-infused orange juice, and maraschino cherry juice into a cocktail shaker and fill it with ice (you might have to make this in two batches). Shake for about 1 minute.

3. Pour the contents of the shaker into four tiki-inspired glasses filled with ice.

4. Garnish each cocktail with a sprig of thyme, a wedge of grilled pineapple on a cocktail pick, and top each drink with a small, additional drizzle of maraschino cherry juice, if desired.

HIBISCUS GINGER PUNCH

SERVES 12

We think this cocktail is something special because of the delicious and unique hibiscus syrup addition. Such a versatile ingredient, we've paired it with fresh lime juice, refreshing ginger ale, and a blend of rums to take us back to lazy summer days at the beach.

INGREDIENTS

24 ounces light rum
8 ounces coconut rum
8 ounces ginger simple syrup (see page 16)
4 ounces hibiscus syrup*
3 limes, juiced
24 ounces ginger ale

GARNISH

Lime wheels, from 2 limes (see page 14)

1. Pour the rum, syrups, and lime juice into a large punch bowl and stir together.

2. Add ice to the punch bowl and stir. Top with the ginger ale and stir again.

3. Garnish with lime wheels, ladle into glasses, and serve.

*Hibiscus syrup can be found in specialty stores, supermarkets, and online.

HONEYDEW CUCUMBER AND MINT AGUA FRESCA PUNCH

SERVES 12

Living in Los Angeles, we both get to take advantage of the fun agua fresca vendors that line the city streets most of the year. We love the super-refreshing juices, freshly made that morning. We've made our version with a healthy amount of tequila!

INGREDIENTS

1 small honeydew melon, peeled, seeded, and chopped
3 Persian cucumbers, chopped (or 1 hothouse cucumber)
1 cup granulated sugar
32 ounces water
24 ounces tequila blanco

GARNISH

12 mint sprigs

1. Place the melon, cucumbers, sugar, and water into a blender and blend until smooth.

2. Strain through a fine mesh sieve and pour into a large mason jar. Add the tequila and fill the jar with ice. Shake for 1 minute and then pour into a punch bowl.

3. Ladle the cocktail into twelve half-pint glasses filled with ice.

4. Garnish with mint sprigs. Serve.

MATCHA MILK

SERVES 2

The first time we had matcha . . . our minds were blown. It tastes a little sweet, and gets its bright green color from the fact that you are actually consuming the tea leaf, and not steeping it. Now we bake with matcha all the time, and one of our favorite ways to drink it is with milk.

INGREDIENTS

1 tablespoon matcha powder
8 ounces whole milk
3 ounces Charbay green tea vodka, or any green tea vodka
2 ounces Tuaca

GARNISH

2 fresh raspberries

1. Pour the matcha and milk into a blender and blend until smooth.

2. Pour the vodka and Tuaca into a cocktail shaker. Add the contents of the blender and fill it with ice. Shake vigorously for about 1 minute.

3. Pour into two double old fashioned glasses filled with ice.

4. Garnish with fresh raspberries. Serve.

MINT JULEP
SERVES 2

We were both lucky enough to experience our first mint julep in Louisville, Kentucky during a business trip. We went as the weather was just beginning to get hot and sticky and these refreshing cocktails were one of the only things keeping us cool—and after the first night we were totally hooked!

INGREDIENTS
6 ounces bourbon
4 ounces mint simple syrup (see page 16)
1½ lemons, juiced
1 teaspoon powdered sugar

GARNISH
Lemon wedges, from 1 lemon (see page 14)
2 mint sprigs

1. Place the bourbon, syrup, and lemon juice into a small pitcher and stir them together. Place the mixture in the refrigerator for at least an hour.

2. Fill two julep glasses with crushed ice and sprinkle 1/2 teaspoon of powdered sugar over each.

3. Pour the julep mixture over the sugar and stir.

4. Garnish with lemon wedges and fresh sprigs of mint. Serve.

MINTED SWEET TEA
SERVES 8

There is nothing we love more than sitting outside with an iced tea, breathing in the fresh air. This is our ideal sweet tea made with mint and sweet tea vodka. The perfect balance for maximum refreshment.

INGREDIENTS
24 ounces sweet tea vodka
16 ounces iced tea
8 ounces mint simple syrup (see page 16)
8 ounces fresh lemon juice
8 ounces fresh orange juice

GARNISH
Lemon wheels, from 2 lemons (see page 14)
24 mint leaves

1. Fill a 64-ounce mason jar with the vodka, iced tea, syrup, lemon juice, and orange juice. Add ice, screw the lid on tightly, and shake for 1 minute.

2. Pour the tea cocktail into eight Collins glasses, garnish each glass with mint leaves and lemon wheels, and serve.

PINEAPPLE-KEY LIME PARADISE

SERVES 4

The tartness of the freshly squeezed key lime juice mixed with the mildly sweet basil simple syrup creates a crazy-awesome combo that's light and refreshing. Perfect for hot summer days by the pool!

INGREDIENTS

8 ounces white rum
6 ounces pineapple juice
4 ounces key lime juice*
2 ounces coconut rum
2 ounces basil simple syrup (see page 16)

GARNISH

8 basil leaves
Key lime wheels, from 2 limes (see page 14)

1. Pour all of the ingredients into a cocktail shaker and fill it with ice (you might have to make this in two batches). Shake for about 1 minute.

2. Pour the mixture into juice glasses filled with ice, and add fresh basil leaves. Garnish with lime wheels on cocktail picks. Serve.

*Key lime juice is available premade, but it's always best to juice it fresh if key limes are available. About 10 key limes are needed for 4 ounces of juice.

PLUOT CAIPIROSKA

SERVES 4

A variation in itself, the caipiroska is another version of the popular Brazilian cocktail the caipirinha, made with vodka instead of cachaça. We've made ours with pluots because we love their sweet flavor and gorgeous, two-toned flesh. If you can't find pluots, no problem. Fresh plums, any variety of your choice, work great for this recipe too!

INGREDIENTS

2 pluots, seeded and chopped
12 mint leaves
2 limes, juiced
2 tablespoons granulated sugar, divided
12 ounces vodka
12 ounces tonic water (or coconut flavored sparkling water)

GARNISH

4 mint sprigs

1. Divide the chopped pluots, mint, and lime juice between four half-pint glasses. Add 1½ teaspoons of sugar to each glass and muddle together.

2. Fill each glass with ice and top with the vodka, then the tonic water. Stir.

3. Garnish each with a sprig of mint. Serve.

PIMM'S CUP

SERVES 4

We love drinking this old school cocktail in hot weather. Its delicious sweet and spicy liqueur makes this drink so refreshing. Perfect for summer!

INGREDIENTS

8 ounces Pimm's No. 1
2 lemons, juiced
12 ounces ginger beer

GARNISH

4 Persian cucumber strips, about ⅛-inch thick*

1. Divide the Pimm's and lemon juice evenly among four Collins glasses and stir.

2. Fill each glass with ice and finish each cocktail with ginger beer.

3. Garnish with skewered cucumber strips and lemon wedges, if using. Serve.

*Fill a small pot with water and bring to a boil. While waiting for the water to boil, make an ice bath by pouring 2 cups of ice and 4 cups of water into a mixing bowl. Carefully drop the cucumber strips into the boiling water and boil for 30 to 45 seconds. Using tongs, gently remove the strips from the pot and drop into the ice bath. Once the strips have cooled completely, skewer them onto long cocktail picks.

RASPBERRY MOJITO

SERVES 4

We remember first seeing someone drinking a Mojito when we were visiting a sweltering New York. We asked to find out what on earth she was drinking and it was a Mojito. You can't miss them—a tall glass filled to the brim with ice, mint, and limes. We've added raspberries to ours to mix things up a bit.

INGREDIENTS

20 raspberries
12 mint leaves
4 teaspoons granulated sugar
8 ounces light rum
2 limes, juiced
24 ounces club soda

GARNISH

16 mint leaves

1. Line up four highball glasses. Divide the raspberries, mint, and sugar amongst the glasses and muddle together in each glass.

2. Add ice and top with the rum, lime juice, and club soda. Stir.

3. Garnish with mint leaves. Serve.

ROASTED STRAWBERRY AND JALAPEÑO FREEZER

SERVES 4

Roasted strawberries are something we both LOVE! Roasting them before freezing them adds a depth of flavor that pairs so well with spicy jalapeños. The candied jalapeño knot garnish is a fun surprise, with bursts of sweet, spicy, and crunchy; it's a total party in your mouth!

INGREDIENTS

2 pounds strawberries, hulled and sliced in half
2 tablespoons champagne vinegar (optional)
1½ tablespoons extra virgin olive oil
12 ounces tequila blanco
6 ounces coconut rum
6 ounces jalapeño simple syrup (see page 16)
2 limes, juiced

GARNISH

2 strawberries, hulled and halved
4 candied jalapeño knots (see page 83 for recipe)

(CONTINUED)

1. Preheat the oven to 375°F.

2. Spread the strawberries onto a baking sheet and drizzle them with the vinegar, if using, and oil. Toss them together and roast for 30 to 40 minutes.

3. Allow the strawberries to cool. Pour the strawberries into a parchment-lined baking dish and place it in the freezer.

4. Once the strawberries are fully frozen (about 3 hours), place them in a blender with the remaining ingredients and blend until smooth. Pour the mixture into four snifter or hurricane glasses.

5. Garnish each glass with a candied jalapeño knot and strawberry skewered on a cocktail pick. Serve.

CANDIED JALAPEÑO KNOTS

INGREDIENTS

1 large jalapeño pepper
1 cup water
1½ cups granulated sugar

1. Stem, seed, and thinly slice the jalapeño into long strips (about ¼-inch thick).

2. Pour the water and sugar into a shallow pan and place it over medium heat, stirring until the sugar dissolves.

3. Lower the heat to medium-low and add the jalapeño strips. Allow them to cook for 1 hour.

4. Preheat the oven to 200°F. Remove the strips with a slotted spoon and tie each one into a loose knot.

5. Place the knots onto a baking sheet (lined with a cooling rack) and put them into the oven. Allow the knots to dry out, with the oven door slightly ajar, for 4 to 6 hours.

6. Remove the knots from the oven and allow them to cool completely.

SKINNY MARGARITA
SERVES 4

We love skinny margaritas, even if they remind us of bad reality television. Popularized by reality-star-turned-business-mogul Bethenny Frankel, the skinny margarita is just what you need to take the edge off of a long day, without drowning yourself in liquid calories.

INGREDIENTS

8 ounces tequila blanco
2 ounces Grand Marnier, or any orange liqueur
2 limes, juiced
16 ounces diet tonic water

GARNISH

Lime wedges, from 1 lime (see page 14)

1. Place the tequila, Grand Marnier, and lime juice into a cocktail shaker filled with ice. Shake for 1 minute.

2. Fill four old fashioned glasses with ice (or you can place one giant ice cube into each glass) and pour the contents of the shaker into each glass. Top each margarita with diet tonic water.

3. Garnish each cocktail with lime wedges. Serve.

STRAWBERRY BASIL AND WHITE WINE SANGRIA

SERVES 4

Although less common than its red counterpart, the white sangria is fresh and even more diverse. We've infused ours with an awesome blend of strawberries and sweet basil, perfect for weekend brunches.

INGREDIENTS

1 lemon, thinly sliced
1 pound strawberries, hulled and thinly sliced
2 cups basil leaves, loosely packed
1 (750ml) bottle Sauvignon Blanc

1. Place the lemon slices, half of the strawberries, and half of the basil in a large pitcher and fill it with the wine. Refrigerate for at least 1 hour and up to 6 hours.

2. Fill half to two-thirds of another large pitcher with ice. Then add the remaining strawberries and basil.

3. Strain the infused wine into the prepared pitcher and stir. Pour the sangria into four stemless white wine glasses. Serve.

AUTUMN RECIPES

When the sweltering summer comes to an end, and it's finally a little chilly in Los Angeles, we do a happy dance—Yayayaya! Time to bring out the autumn spices that define this totally rad aromatic season and pop them into some cocktails! From our cozy **Apple Pie Cider** to our ginger-kissed **Roasted Pear Delight**, these robust drinks will give you a bit of autumn in every sip.

APPLE PIE CIDER

SERVES 4

Bring on the apple pies! That is what autumn is all about. We took our love for apples pies and condensed it into a cocktail by including all the spices you find in this classic dessert. This is our go-to drink when it's time to curl up in our pajamas in front of the fireplace.

INGREDIENTS

16 ounces apple cider
1 orange, juiced
1 teaspoon vanilla extract
1 lemon, peel only and pith removed
½-inch piece fresh ginger, peeled
2 cinnamon sticks
4 whole cloves
2 tablespoons unsalted butter, softened
1 tablespoon light brown sugar
8 ounces bourbon

GARNISH

4 apple "stars", from 1 to 2 apples, (any variety)*

*Cut the apple into ¼-inch slices. Then, using a 1½ to 2-inch circle cutter, cut circles out of the center of the slices. Remove any remaining seeds.

(CONTINUED)

1. Place the cider, orange juice, vanilla, lemon peel, ginger, cinnamon sticks, and cloves in a medium saucepan and simmer for about 10 minutes. Remove from the heat, cover, and steep for 1 hour. Strain and set aside.

2. In a small bowl, mash together the butter and sugar until thoroughly mixed.

3. Place the cider mixture over medium heat and bring to a boil. Stir in the butter mixture and continue to stir until melted and fully incorporated. Remove the saucepan from the heat and stir in the bourbon.

4. Pour the cider into four mugs and top with the apple "stars." Serve.

ROASTED PEAR DELIGHT

SERVES 4

This drink has a combination of cocktail flavors we just love: pear, lemon, and ginger. The pear ball garnish is a cute little finish to these deliciously dainty drinks.

INGREDIENTS

6 Bosc pears, peeled, cored, and chopped

2 tablespoons light brown sugar

2 tablespoons unsalted butter, melted

1 lemon, juiced

4 ounces vodka

2 ounces Domaine de Canton, or any ginger liqueur

GARNISH

12 Bosc pear balls (about 2 pears)*

*Peel the pears and use a ¼-inch melon baller to make the balls. Dip them in lemon juice to avoid browning.

(CONTINUED)

1. Preheat oven to 375°F.

2. Place the chopped pears, brown sugar, and butter in a medium mixing bowl and toss them together until well combined. Spread the mixture onto a baking sheet, in a single layer, and bake in the oven for 15 to 20 minutes.

3. Transfer the roasted pears to a blender, add the lemon juice, and blend until smooth. Strain the mixture through a fine sieve lined with cheese-cloth, and place the juice in the refrigerator until chilled (1 to 2 hours).

4. Pour the roasted pear juice, vodka, and Domaine de Canton into a cocktail shaker and fill it with ice (you might have to make this in two batches). Shake for about 1 minute and set aside.

5. Using a ¼-inch melon baller, make pear balls from a freshly peeled pear. Set out four coupe glasses and drop 3 pear balls into each glass.

6. Reshake the cocktail mixture and strain into each glass over the balls. Serve.

ASIAN PEAR KAMIKAZE

SERVES 2

The mild flavor of the Asian pear makes these drinks so easy to throw back. The matchstick garnish is a fun and different way to serve these popular cocktails.

INGREDIENTS

4 ounces vodka
4 ounces Koval Asian Pear Liqueur, or any Asian pear liqueur
4 ounces Asian pear juice*

GARNISH

Asian pear matchsticks, from 1 Asian pear**
2 apple mint sprigs

1. Place all of the ingredients in a cocktail shaker and fill it with ice. Shake for about 1 minute.

2. Pour the mixture into two old fashioned glasses filled with ice and finish with Asian pear matchsticks and sprigs of mint. Serve.

*You can find premade Asian pear juice at Asian markets. Or, you can make your own: Peel, core, and chop 3 large fresh Asian pears (found at most supermarkets), and blend them with the juice of 1 lemon. Then strain the mixture and use the remaining juice.

**Cut the pear into 2- to 3-inch long sticks (⅛-inch thickness).

BANANAS FOSTER

SERVES 2

This richly decadent drink is definitely splurge-worthy in our book. Bananas Foster is one of those desserts we must get if we see it on any menu. We transformed it into a delicious cocktail and it is now one of our new favorite incarnations.

INGREDIENTS
1 cup caramel ice cream
8 ounces whole milk
6 ounces Bols Crème de Banane, or any crème de banane
2 ounces Kilkenny Butterscotch Liqueur,
*   or any butterscotch liqueur*
1 banana, peeled

GARNISH
Whipped cream
Caramel sauce

1. Place all of the ingredients into a blender and blend until smooth.

2. Set out two half-pint glasses and pour the mixture into each of the glasses, distributing evenly.

3. Top each drink with whipped cream and finish with a drizzle of caramel sauce. Serve.

CLASSIC MARTINI

SERVES 2

A classic American cocktail, left untouched. Our only recommendation is to dirty it up with some pickle juice if you're craving both a little old and a little new. Done deal!

INGREDIENTS
6 ounces gin
1 ounce dry vermouth

GARNISH
Pitted and stuffed green olives
Lemon twists (see page 14)
Pickled pearled onions
Gherkins

1. Pour the gin and vermouth into a cocktail shaker and fill it with ice. Shake for about 1 minute.

2. Strain and pour into two cocktail glasses. Finish with your garnish of choice. Serve.

HOP SKIP AND GO NAKED

SERVES 4

A popular cocktail among college students, the strong citrus notes blended with the unassuming light beer create a fun drink that is easy to sip.

INGREDIENTS

8 ounces citrus vodka
4 lemons, juiced
4 ounces lemon-lime soda
4 ounces light beer

GARNISH

Lemon wheels, from 1 lemon (see page 14)

1. Pour all of the ingredients into a cocktail shaker and fill it with ice (you might have to make this in two batches). Shake for about 1 minute.

2. Strain the mixture into four old fashioned glasses.

3. Garnish with lemon wheels skewered on cocktail picks. Serve.

ORANGE LICORICE WHIP
SERVES 2

This cocktail is definitely for the licorice-loving folk. The orange flavor paired with the anisette lightens this striking drink, creating an overall smooth cocktail.

INGREDIENTS
8 dashes orange bitters
4 ounces vodka
2 ounces anisette
2 ounces Grand Marnier, or any orange liqueur

GARNISH
2 orange twists, from 1 orange (see page 14)

1. Add a few dashes of orange bitters to the bottoms of two martini glasses.

2. Pour the vodka and anisette into a cocktail shaker and fill it with ice. Shake for 1 minute.

3. Strain into the martini glasses, over the orange bitters, and top each glass with Grand Marnier.

4. Garnish each glass with an orange twist. Serve.

PEAR & BUBBLES

SERVES 6

We are both huge bubbly-drink fans, and whenever we go out for lunch we now both get something bubbly to wash down our meals. It is so nice in the middle of the afternoon because it's not loaded down with sugar. Drink up!

INGREDIENTS

6 Bosc pears, peeled and chopped
1½ tablespoons light brown sugar
½ teaspoon ground cinnamon
Pinch ground cardamom
½ lemon, juiced
1 (750ml) bottle sparkling wine or Champagne, chilled

GARNISH

24 Bosc pear balls, made from about 4 pears*
   (see page 108)
½ lemon, juiced
6 Bosc pear stars, made from about 2 pears**
   (see page 108)

(CONTINUED)

1. Preheat a broiler to low setting.

2. Place the pears, brown sugar, cinnamon, and cardamom onto a baking sheet and toss together until the pears are well coated.

3. Place the baking sheet under the broiler for 3 to 4 minutes or until the pears begin to caramelize.

4. Pour the caramelized pears into a blender and add the lemon juice. Purée until smooth.

5. Strain the mixture and chill the juice for at least 30 minutes and up to 1 hour.

6. Divide the pear juice between six champagne flute glasses and top each with the sparkling wine or champagne.

7. To finish, drop 4 pear balls into each glass and top with a pear star. Serve.

*Peel the pears and use a ¼-inch melon baller to make the balls. Dip them in lemon juice to avoid browning.

**Cut about a ¼-inch slice from the side of the pear (with the skin on). Place the slice, cut side down, onto a cutting board and cut into about ¼-inch slices. Repeat until you have at least 18 slices. Dip them in the lemon juice (to avoid browning) and set aside. Then cut a ½-inch slice from the pear. Using a ¼-inch circle cutter, or piping tip, punch out 6 circles. Carefully skewer 3 pear slices onto a cocktail pick, and finish with 1 small pear circle.

TAMARIND MARGARITA

SERVES 4

The tamarind margarita is a special kind of margarita that we totally crush on each time we see it on a menu. Although margaritas are typically a cooling, summertime cocktail, this tamarind margarita is perfect for heading into autumn. It has a distinct bittersweet taste that creates a warming sensation. And our honey, salt, cayenne, and cinnamon-blended rim is as addicting as the cocktail itself!

INGREDIENTS

½ cup honey
½ cup kosher salt
2 tablespoons cayenne pepper
½ teaspoon ground cinnamon
6 ounces tamarind simple syrup (see page 16)
8 ounces reposado tequila
2 ounces Grand Marnier, or any orange liqueur
2 oranges, juiced
1 lime, juiced

GARNISH

Lime wedges, from 1 lime (see page 14)
4 mint sprigs

(CONTINUED)

1. Spread the honey onto a plate in a thin layer. Combine the salt, cayenne, and cinnamon on another plate and stir with a fork until completely combined.

2. Rim four old fashioned glasses with a thin layer of honey, followed by the salt mixture. Set the prepared glasses aside until ready to use.

3. Place all of the remaining ingredients into a cocktail shaker and fill it with ice (you might have to make this in two batches). Shake for about 1 minute.

4. Pour the mixture into prepared glasses filled with ice.

5. Garnish with lime wedges and mint leaves. Serve.

PRINCETON

SERVES 4

We were not initially drawn to this classic cocktail by the delicious flavors, but by the neat layering effect the port and gin have against one another. Stun your guests at your next cocktail party with this super easy, yet impressive, martini!

INGREDIENTS

8 dashes orange bitters
8 ounces gin
8 ounces port

1. Set out four martini glasses and add a couple dashes of bitters into the bottom of each glass.

2. Pour the gin into each glass and then carefully pour the port into each glass—from the side— to create a layering effect. Serve.

THYME OLD FASHIONED
SERVES 4

This cocktail always makes us think of a group of men playing cards and smoking cigars while sipping on this manly beverage. We've added a hint of sweetness to our version with just a splash of pomegranate juice, which is perfect with the savory thyme infusion. A classic cocktail revamped and looking cute!

INGREDIENTS
8 ounces bourbon
6 ounces thyme simple syrup (see page 16)
6 ounces fresh orange juice
2 ounces pomegranate juice

GARNISH
4 fresh thyme sprigs

1. Distribute the bourbon, syrup, and orange juice evenly among four old fashioned glasses. Stir.

2. Fill each glass with ice and top each drink with a splash of pomegranate juice.

3. Garnish drinks with sprigs of thyme and serve.

VANILLA BEAN IRISH COFFEE

SERVES 4

Sometimes it's better not to overcomplicate something that's already awesome, so we've kept our version of Irish coffee simple. We've infused the flavor of natural vanilla into the cocktail and topped it with a light and frothy cream.

INGREDIENTS

1 vanilla bean
1 tablespoon powdered sugar
8 ounces strong black coffee, hot
12 ounces Kahlúa, or any coffee liqueur
10 ounces heavy cream, partially whipped

1. Slice the vanilla bean in half lengthwise and scrape the seeds from the pod. Stir the vanilla seeds and sugar into the coffee until the sugar dissolves.

2. Divide the coffee into four mug tumblers, or regular mugs, and add the Kahlúa to each.

3. Top each glass with partially whipped cream and gently stir. Serve.

WINTER RECIPES

Bundling up in winter coats, boots, and scarves is one of our favorite delights. But that doesn't mean that once we come in from the cold, we don't want to be warmed up with some cozy cocktails! From the festive **Star Gimlet** to the sophisticated **Gentleman**, these satisfying drinks will be the perfect nightcap for those cold winter nights.

BLOODY BULLEIT

SERVES 4

When blood oranges begin to pop up during their short season, we get really excited! And we love pairing them with the sweet and smoky flavor of Bulleit Rye American Whiskey. This cocktail is so simple and so good—it's definitely one of our favorites!

INGREDIENTS

8 ounces Bulleit Rye American Whiskey

2 ounces orange syrup*

2 blood oranges, juiced

1 lemon, juiced

12 ounces club soda

GARNISH

4 blood orange half wheels, from 1 blood orange (see page 14)

1. Place all of the ingredients, except the club soda, into a cocktail shaker and fill it with ice (you might have to make this in two batches). Shake for about 1 minute.

2. Pour into four old fashioned glasses filled with ice and top with the club soda. Finish with blood orange half wheels. Serve.

*Orange syrup can be found in specialty stores, supermarkets, and online.

SWEET CARDAMOM BOURBON MILK PUNCH

SERVES 10

This is one of our all-time favorite brunch drinks. We absolutely love sipping on this spiced sweet milk punch when we know we're about to indulge and devour a huge savory breakfast.

INGREDIENTS

36 ounces whole milk
12 ounces bourbon
8 ounces brandy
⅔ cup light brown sugar
4 ounces Tuaca
2 tablespoons vanilla extract
15 cardamom pods
3 star anise
2 cinnamon sticks

GARNISH

Freshly grated nutmeg

(CONTINUED)

1. Pour all of the ingredients into a large saucepan and stir together. Simmer over medium heat for 10 to 15 minutes or until the sugar dissolves.

2. Remove from the heat, cover, and steep for 1 hour. Place the punch in the refrigerator until completely chilled (1 to 2 hours).

3. Strain the mixture through a fine sieve lined with cheesecloth and ladle the punch into ten milk punch cups filled with ice.

4. Sprinkle each cup with a dash of freshly grated nutmeg. Serve.

FROZEN PEPPERMINT HOT CHOCOLATE

SERVES 2

This drink was inspired by the frozen hot chocolate from the popular Serendipity restaurant in NYC. We really love how whimsical all the menu items seem at Serendipity—especially the frozen hot chocolate—and like to think of this cocktail as the peppermint, grown-up version of that well-known drink.

INGREDIENTS

12 ounces whole milk
4 ounces milk chocolate, finely chopped
2 ounces semisweet chocolate, finely chopped
6 ounces peppermint schnapps
1 heaping cup mint chocolate chip ice cream
1 cup ice

Sweetened whipped cream:

1 cup heavy whipping cream
¼ cup superfine sugar
1 teaspoon vanilla extract

GARNISH

Shaved dark chocolate, about 1 ounce
Chopped peppermint candy, about 2 tablespoons

(CONTINUED)

1. Place the milk into a small saucepan and place over medium-low heat to scald. Stir in both the milk and semisweet chocolate, and continue to stir until completely melted. Remove from the heat and set aside until cooled (about 30 minutes). Then place in the refrigerator until chilled (about 1 hour).

2. While the hot chocolate chills, make the sweetened whipped cream: Place all of the ingredients for the whipped cream into a mixing bowl and whip with an electric hand mixer until stiff peaks form. Place in the refrigerator until ready to use.

3. Place the chilled hot chocolate and the peppermint schnapps, ice cream, and ice into a blender and blend until smooth. Pour the mixture into two mugs and top with whipped cream.

4. Garnish each drink with a sprinkle of shaved chocolate and chopped peppermint candy. Serve.

CLASSIC COSMOPOLITAN
SERVES 2

We first heard of this cocktail from *Sex and the City*, and like most of our friends had never had it before. This martini is just a little fruity and sweet, which is perfect when you don't want a crazy sugary drink.

INGREDIENTS
6 ounces vodka
4 ounces cranberry juice
1 lime, juiced

GARNISH
Lime twists, from 1 lime (see page 14)

1. Place all of the ingredients into a cocktail shaker and fill it with ice. Shake for about 1 minute.

2. Strain the mixture into two cocktail glasses and garnish with lime twists. Serve.

CLUBCAR

SERVES 2

One of our friends is actually the mastermind behind this sidecar variation. After running out of orange liqueur one night, he quickly improvised with a bit of Chambord, in addition to a splash of tonic water. That night, the delicious and now ever popular (in our household at least!) Clubcar was born.

INGREDIENTS

5 ounces cognac
1 lemon, juiced
8 ounces tonic water
2 ounces Chambord

GARNISH

2 lemon twists, from 2 lemons (see page 14)

1. Pour the cognac, lemon juice, and tonic water into two old fashioned glasses filled with ice and stir.

2. Top each with a drizzle of Chambord and finish with a lemon twist. Serve.

NEAT NEGRONI
SERVES 4

Sometimes you just want to sip on a cocktail without dealing with all the ice. This cocktail is an example of a tasty, classic cocktail that's usually shaken with ice, but we've changed it up by serving it nice and neat to avoid any diluting of this bold drink!

INGREDIENTS
6 ounces gin
6 ounces Campari
6 ounces sweet vermouth

GARNISH
Tangerine wheels, from 1 tangerine (see page 14)

1. Place all of the ingredients into a cocktail shaker and shake for about 1 minute.

2. Pour into four half-pint or old fashioned glasses.

3. Garnish with tangerine wheels. Serve neat.

STAR GIMLET

SERVES 4

We always feel very "Mad Men" when we order one of these. This old school cocktail is both sweet and sharp, and misty-looking because of the lime juice. It's our go-to drink when we are with a couple of friends and want to sit, sip, and relax.

INGREDIENTS
8 ounces gin
4 ounces St-Germain, or any elderflower liqueur
2 ounces passion fruit syrup*
2 limes, juiced

GARNISH
4 star fruit slices, made from 1 to 2 star fruits**

1. Pour all of the ingredients into a cocktail shaker filled with ice and shake for about 1 minute. Pour into four old fashioned glasses or snifters (for a fun change) filled with ice.

2. Garnish the rim of each glass with a star fruit slice. Serve.

*Passion fruit syrup can be found in specialty stores, supermarkets, and online.

**Cut the ends off of each star fruit, and cut into about ⅛-inch slices. Remove any seeds.

TANGERINE 'N' CREAM
SERVES 2

This flavor combination dates back to our childhood when we would get the treat of going out for Orange Juliuses at the infamous juice bar chain of the same name. The original drink had a delicious blend of orange juice, milk, vanilla, sugar, and ice. It's the inspiration for this sweet, nostalgic cocktail made with tangerines and a hint of vanilla.

INGREDIENTS
8 tangerines, juiced (about 6 ounces juice)
4 ounces vodka
4 ounces heavy cream
1½ teaspoons powdered sugar
1 teaspoon vanilla extract

GARNISH
Tangerine zest, from 1 tangerine

1. Place all of the ingredients into a cocktail shaker and fill it with ice. Shake for about 1 minute.

2. Divide the mixture into two glasses of your choice (each able to hold about 8 oz.) filled with ice and garnish the tops with tangerine zest. Serve.

THE GENTLEMAN

SERVES 4

This drink is sophisticated, striking, unique, and well dressed . . . everything a gentleman should be!

INGREDIENTS

8 ounces Cognac
4 ounces Drambuie
2 lemons, juiced
8 ounces ginger beer

GARNISH

8 fresh golden sage leaves

1. Pour the cognac, Drambuie, and lemon juice into four old fashioned glasses filled with ice. Stir each drink and top with the ginger beer.

2. Garnish with fresh golden sage leaves. Serve.

BROWN SUGAR BUTTERY NIPPLE

SERVES 4

With a name like "buttery nipple," this drink should be playful, decadent, and most importantly, completely delicious. We think we nailed it with our combo of sweet butterscotch schnapps, smooth Irish cream, and half and half, with a rich brown sugar rim—but you be the judge!

INGREDIENTS

½ cup honey
½ cup light brown sugar
8 ounces butterscotch schnapps
8 ounces Baileys Irish cream, or any Irish cream
4 ounces half and half

1. Spread the honey onto a plate in a thin layer. Place the brown sugar on another plate and use a fork to spread it into a thin layer.

2. Rim four double old fashioned glasses with a thin layer of honey, followed by the brown sugar, until fully coated.

3. Pour the schnapps, Baileys, and half and half into a cocktail shaker with ice. Shake for 1 minute.

4. Fill the prepared glasses with ice and pour the contents of the shaker into each glass. Serve.

SWEET CITRUS FIZZ

SERVES 1

Creating a wonderfully fizzy drink with the addition of a simple egg white?! We're totally in! Not only is this fun cocktail visually appealing, it's delicious and super easy to throw together! Win-win!

INGREDIENTS

2 ounces gin
2 lemons, juiced
1 orange, juiced
1 ounce Grand Marnier, or any orange liqueur
1 egg white
½ lime, juiced
1 teaspoon powdered sugar, divided
4 ounces club soda

GARNISH

1 brulèed lemon wheel (see page 144 for recipe)

1. Place all of the ingredients, except the club soda, into a cocktail shaker and fill it with ice. Shake vigorously for 2 to 3 minutes or until the egg white foams into a soft peaked meringue in the shaker.

2. Strain into a Collins glass filled with ice, and top off with club soda. Scoop the excess foam over the top of the drink and garnish with the prepared lemon wheel. Serve.

BRULÉED LEMON WHEEL

INGREDIENTS

1 lemon wheel, from 1 lemon (see page 14)
¼ cup turbinado sugar

1. Place the lemon wheel between layers of paper towels and gently press to remove excess liquid. Remove from the paper towels, and sprinkle half of the sugar generously over the surface, and brulée with a torch (or under a broiler for about 30 seconds) until golden brown and caramelized. Allow to cool completely. Flip over and repeat with remaining sugar. Set aside until ready to use.

GLOSSARY

This glossary is not intended as a comprehensive guide to all things pertaining to cocktails—but instead a helpful guide to the spirits that we've used in this book.

ANISETTE
A colorless, anise-flavored (but licorice-free) liqueur made from distilled aniseed

ASIAN PEAR LIQUEUR
A liqueur infused with the sweet, juicy, and crisp flavor of Asian pears

BAILEYS IRISH CREAM
A popular brand of Irish cream *(see page 148)*

BITTERS
A usually pungent bitter liquor made by steeping botanical extracts. You'll only need a few dashes/drops to add that special touch to your drinks. Increasingly popular, there are now many different flavor varieties available. (We've used orange in a few of our recipes.)

BOLS CRÈME DE BANANE
A popular brand of crème de banane *(see page 147)*

BOURBON
American whiskey, aged in oak barrels, and predominantly made of corn

BRANDY
An alcoholic spirit distilled primarily from grapes

BULLEIT RYE AMERICAN WHISKEY
A popular brand of whiskey *(see page 152)* made from a 95% rye mash

BUTTERSCOTCH LIQUEUR
See Butterscotch Schnapps

BUTTERSCOTCH SCHNAPPS
A liqueur made from a blend of butter, brown sugar, and a neutral spirit

CACHAÇA
A colorless spirit hailing from Brazil, distilled from sugar cane

CAMPARI
A deep red-colored type of strong bitter aperitif containing a blend of alcohol, water, fruit, and herbs

CHAMBORD
Produced in France, a liqueur with a predominant raspberry flavor made with red and black raspberries, cognac, vanilla, citrus peel, and honey

CHARBAY GREEN TEA VODKA
A popular brand of green tea vodka *(see page 152)*

CHARTREUSE
Originally created by Carthusian monks, a green or yellow herbal liqueur distilled from more than 130 plants (the yellow chartreuse is more mild and sweet in flavor)

COFFEE LIQUEUR
A coffee-flavored liqueur that can be made from a variety of different spirits, but is commonly made from rum

COGNAC
French variety of brandy, made with particular varieties of grapes, twice distilling the alcohol in copper pots and aging the spirit for two years in specific French oak barrels

CORDIAL
See Liqueur

CRÈME DE BANANE
A sweet translucent yellow-colored liqueur made from ripened bananas

DOMAINE DE CANTON
A popular brand of ginger liqueur *(see page 148)*

DRAMBUIE
A sweet and smooth liqueur made of Scotch whiskey, honey, herbs, and spices

VODKA
A colorless spirit, historically made from fermented potatoes, but can also be made from other grains, available in a variety of flavors, such as citrus, sweet green tea, and sweet tea

WHISKEY
A spirit made from fermented grain mash (of which there can be many different varieties depending on the type of grain used—each creating their own distinct flavors, colors, and aromas)

YELLOW CHARTREUSE
See Chartreuse

INDEX

DRINKS BY NAME

DRINKS BY PRIMARY ALCOHOLIC INGREDIENT

Tequila

Vodka

Whiskey

Wine

ABOUT THE AUTHORS

Jenny Park and **Teri Lyn Fisher** run the popular food blog **SpoonForkBacon.com**—a site they created together in 2011 as a place for people to find delicious recipes (from appetizers to entrées) paired with beautifully styled photographs. Park, a graduate of the University of California Santa Barbara and Le Cordon Bleu, is a food stylist and recipe writer/developer. Fisher is an enthusiastic home cook and photographer. Some of their clients include HGTV, Food & Wine, and Bon Appetit. Their first book, *Tiny Food Party!*, was named one of Good Morning America's top pick cookbooks in 2012.